I Want to Learn to Fly a Kite

Bahareh Amidi

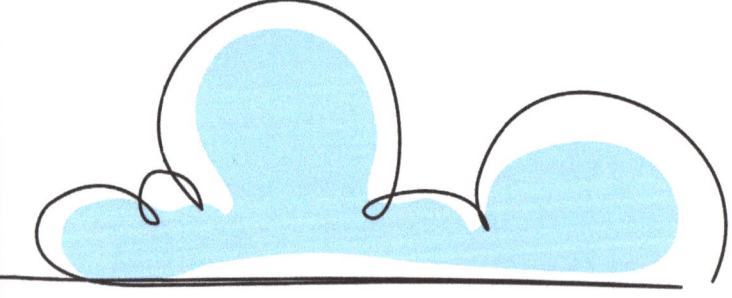

I Want to Learn to Fly a Kite

cover and interior illustrations by
   Adora:
    @AdoraArts

email: connect@bahareh.com
facebook.com/Bahareh.Amidi
twitter.com/BaharehAmidi
youtube.com/baharehLIVE
instagram.com/bahareh_poetess
www.bahareh.com

تو پرواز را بیاموز،
باد را که خوشدر بلد است

— سهراب سپهری

"You just learn to fly —
the wind knows what to do."

— Sohrab Sepehri

Listen to I Want to Learn to Fly a Kite

I am not quite sure
why I would want to learn to fly a kite,
It is not real flight
if you always have a string
attached to one arm
Or seeing it another way,
is it like having a guide leading you along

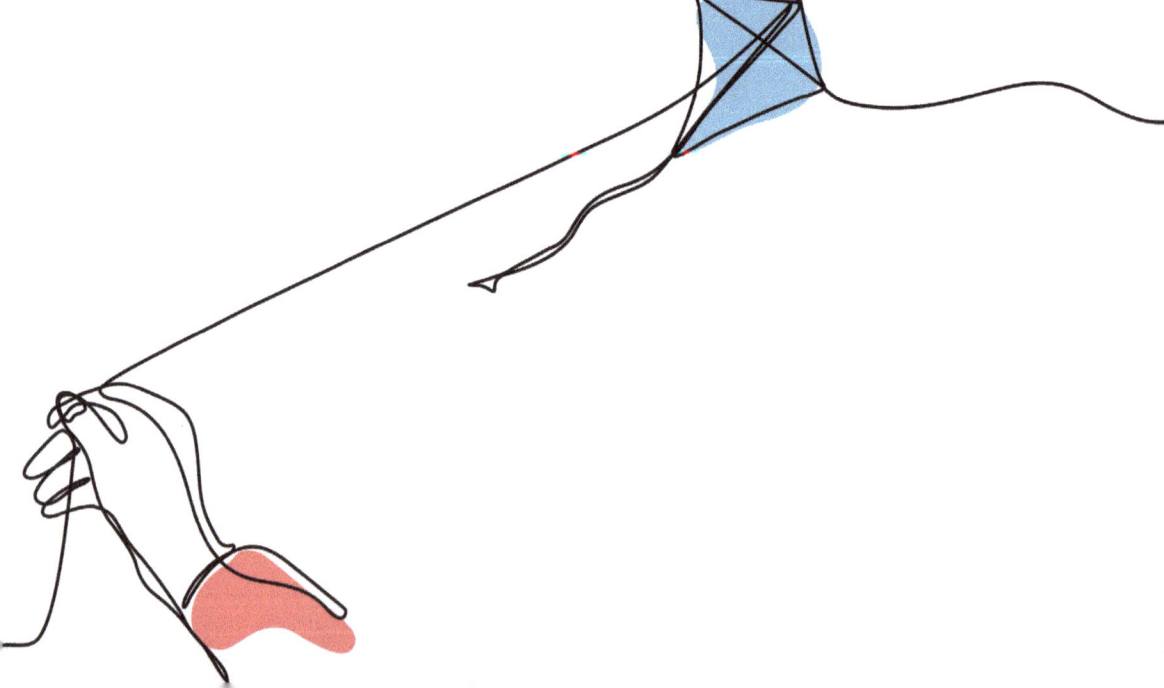

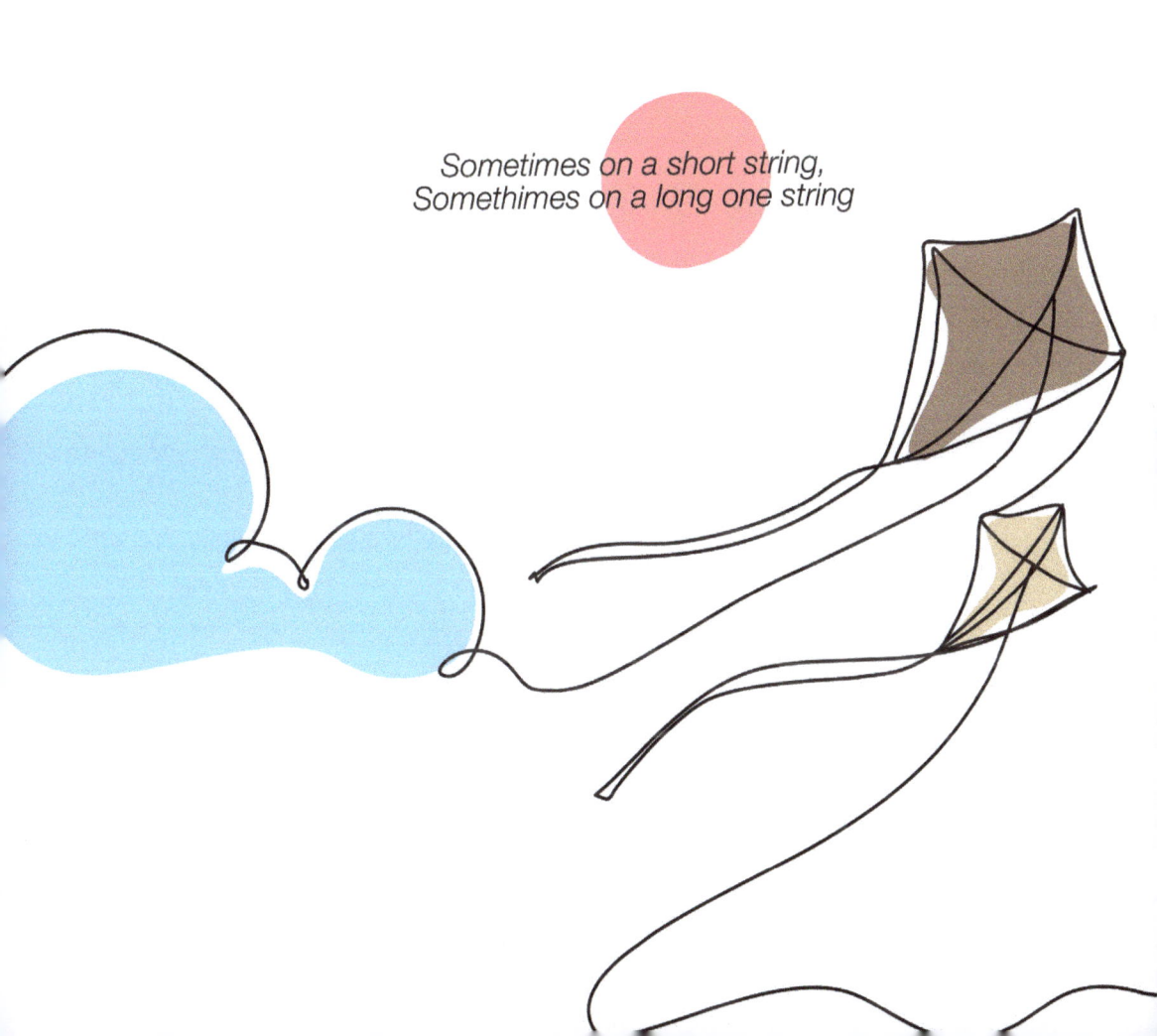

Sometimes on a short string,
Somethimes on a long one string

I wonder
if I wish to be the kite
or to be the one on the ground
holding the strings of the kite
I guess to get a full experience,
it would be ideal for me
to be in the sky
being guided for a while

and then to have my feet rooted
as I guide myself in the sky.

*There is low pressure above the kite
and heavy pressure from underneath the kite.
Is this what is meant by you
are the wind beneath my wings?
Would that be the roar of the lion in the sky
and the buzzing of the bee in the fields?*

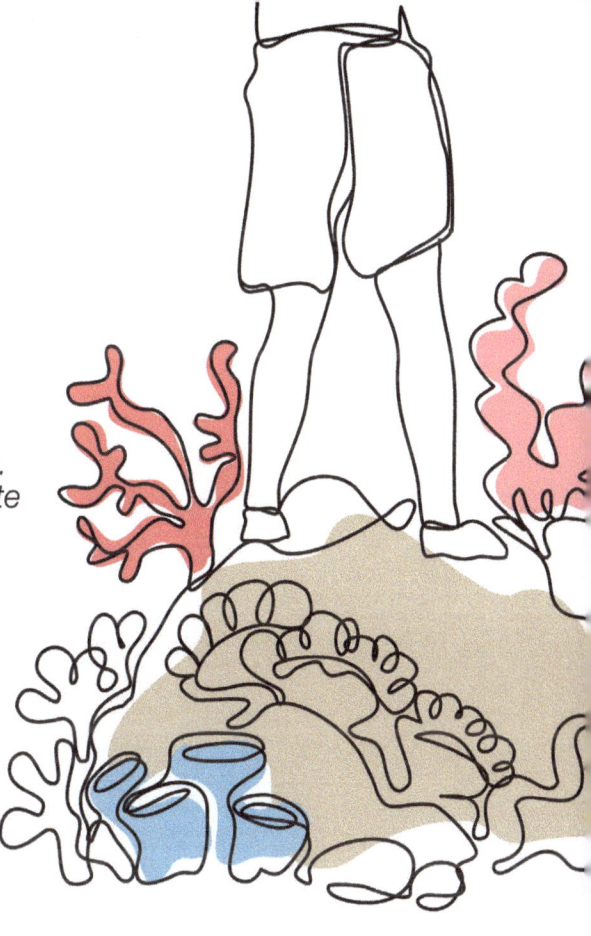

Here I am standing
on the deepest coral reef in the sea.
I am holding a beautiful deep blue kite
with a red gold fish on its tail
I watch as the sharks catch
and eat their prey
and then swim
and smile
and live the rest of the day.
I am a human,
I want to stay under the sea,
where no one will kill me
or use me
or abuse me
or rape me
just because I breathe.
There is no jealousy
for the tusks I carry in my mouth,
nor the diamonds I wear
at the sole of my feet.

I look around
and after all this time of hanging
on to the kite,
I realize I am in a small aquarium
in a small pet shop in a mall.

The lion roaring was in fact the kitten purring.
The shark I thought I saw
was only a plastic image of Jaws being advertised.
The kite was nothing
but a mini balloon the store gives away.
But there was one real being
and that was me holding on to the tail
of the goldfish in the aquarium.

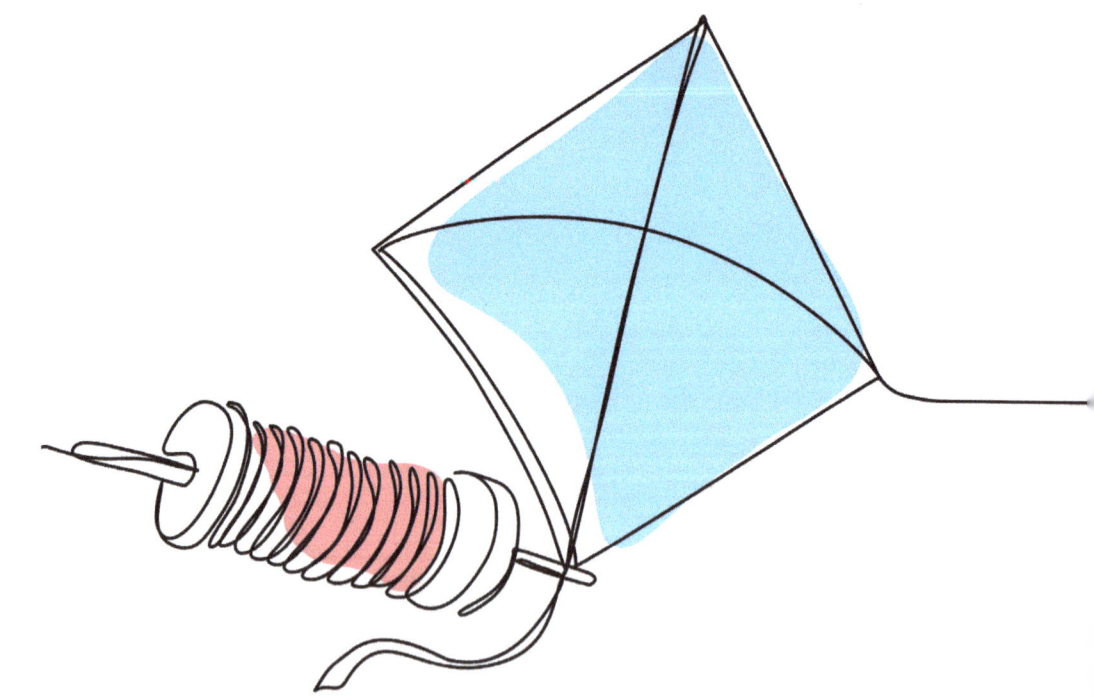

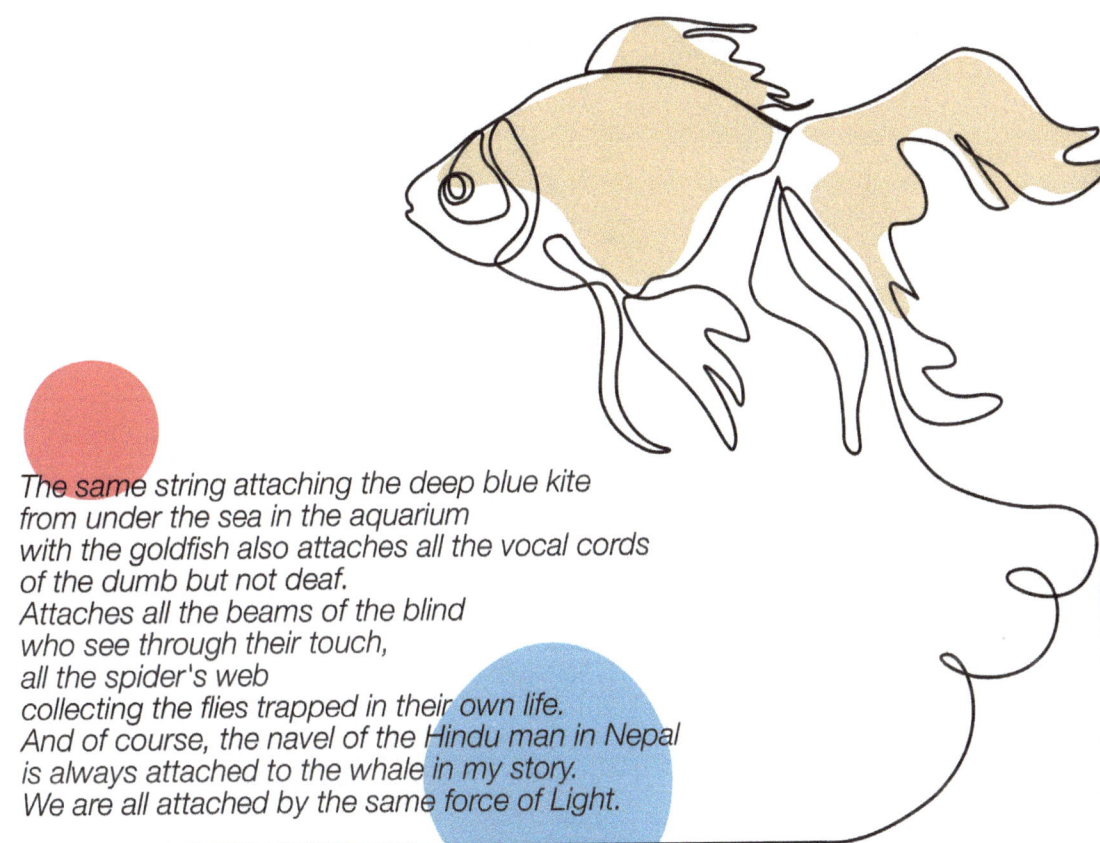

The same string attaching the deep blue kite
from under the sea in the aquarium
with the goldfish also attaches all the vocal cords
of the dumb but not deaf.
Attaches all the beams of the blind
who see through their touch,
all the spider's web
collecting the flies trapped in their own life.
And of course, the navel of the Hindu man in Nepal
is always attached to the whale in my story.
We are all attached by the same force of Light.

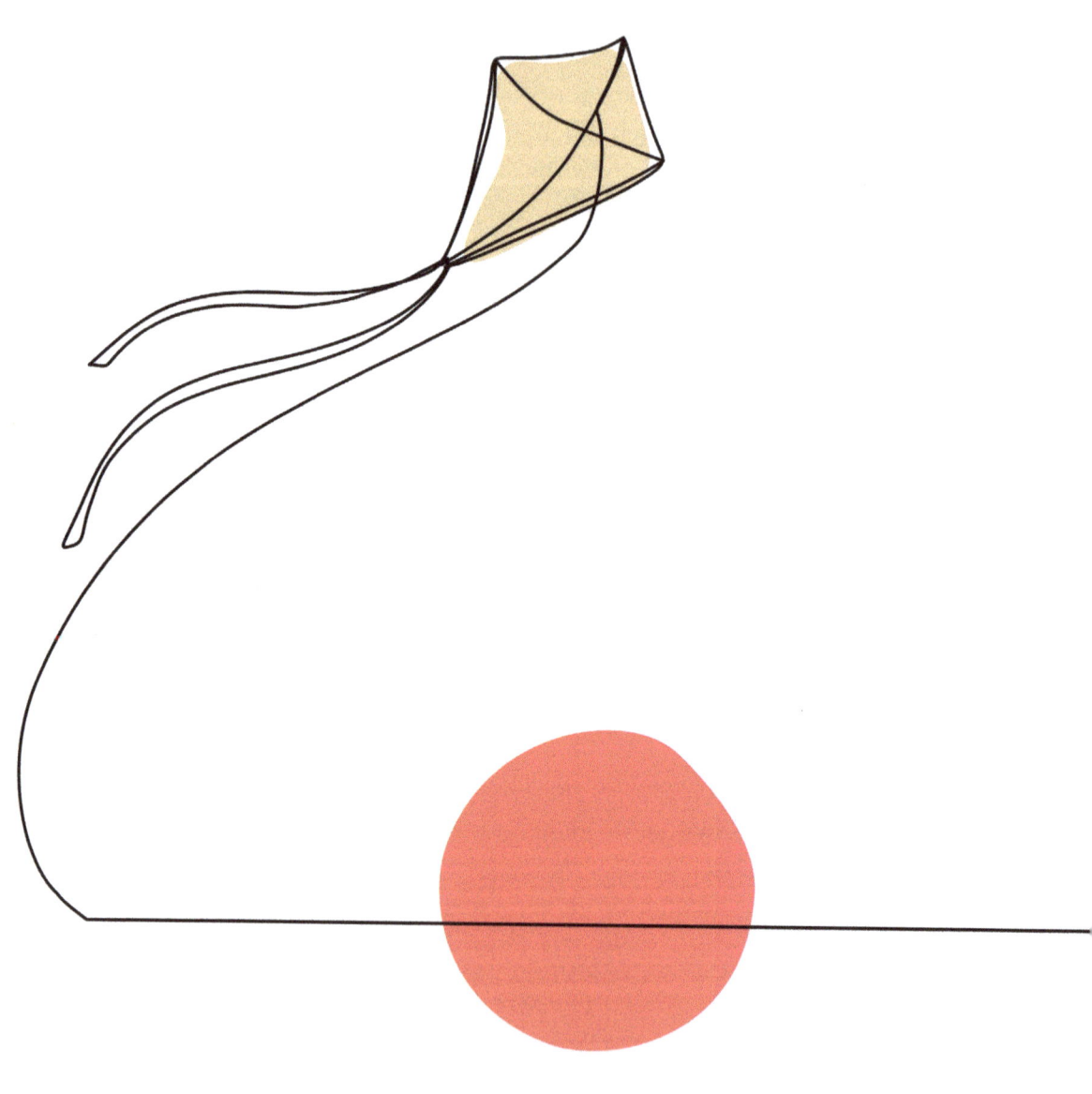

For those souls a bit more advanced in life.
We might be given a kite to fly
to take us away from the place of the rock.
From time to time,
to look upon the kite will remind us
how big we are in God's eyes.

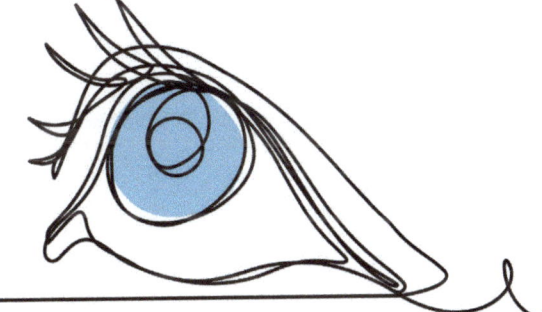

The next morning;
the morning after the night before
when I learned how to say NO,
I woke up to find the most magical kite next to my bed
I know it was there
when I went to bed,
but I did not recognize it as a kite.

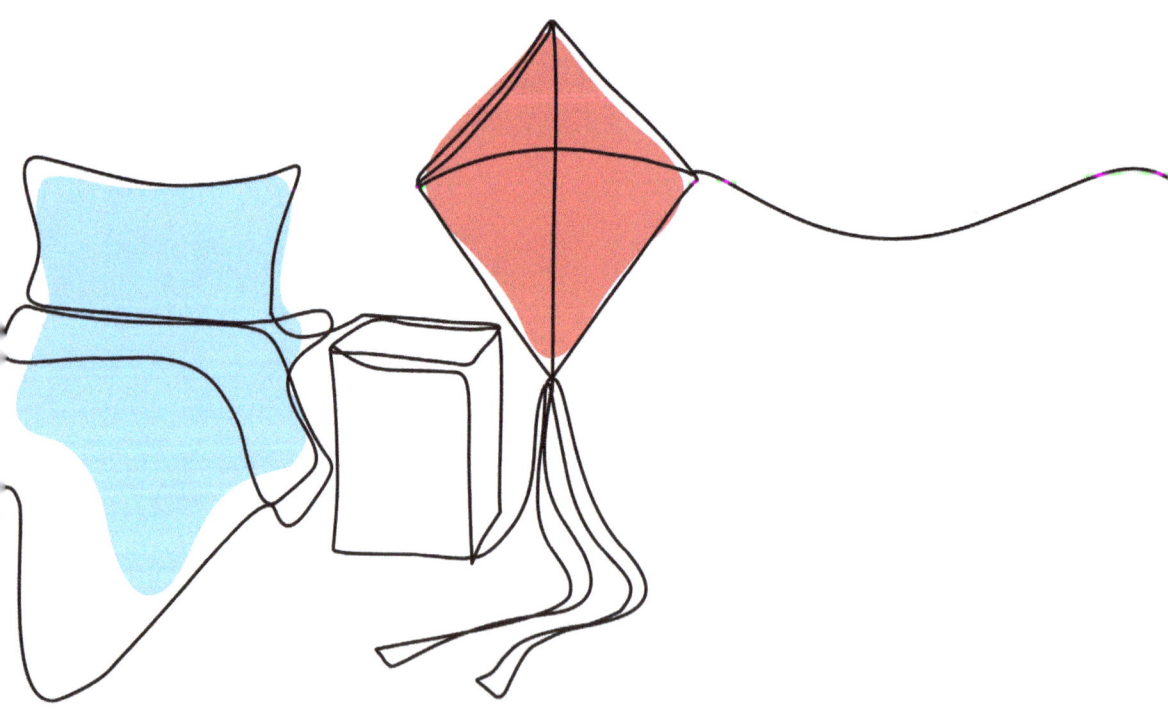

As I slept,
my thoughts and my dreams
must have given life
to the magical paper made out of bark of trees.
My same eyes were willing to see
the possibilities I hold when I am not held on a string.

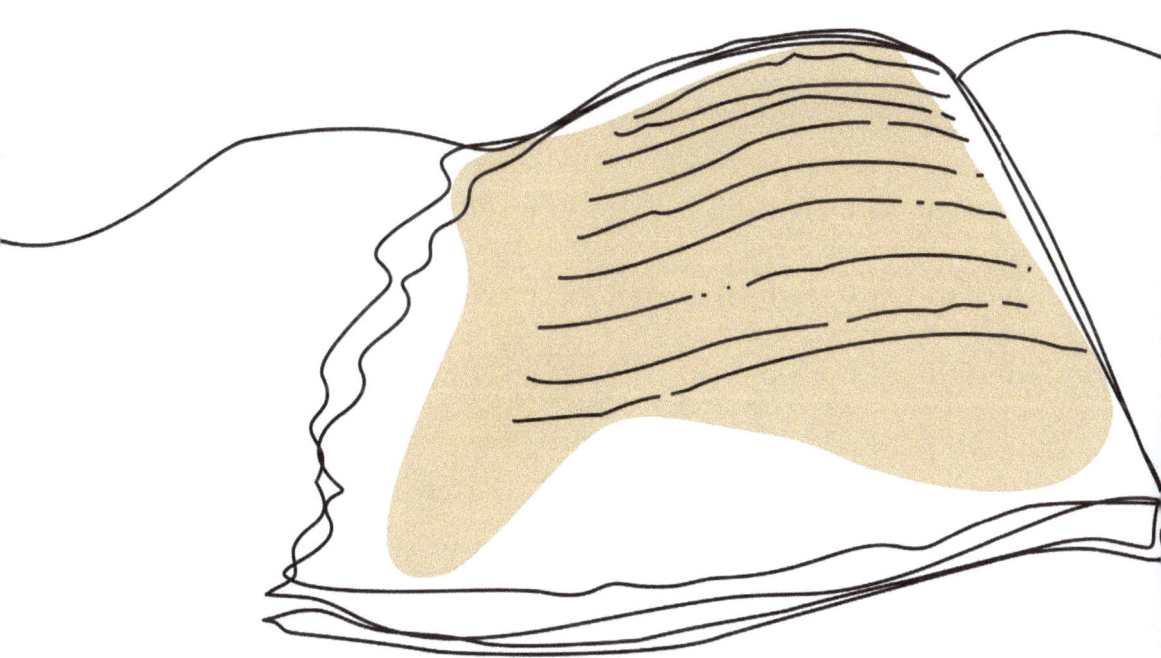

I suddenly see myself as kite runner
and the kite maker
and not necessarily as the kite at all.
If I were the kite
I would always be manipulated
if not by a person as I'd be on a string
then by the wind with the string still attached to my throat.
My throat needs to breathe
My eyes need to see
My voice needs to be heard.
I am no longer a part of the herd

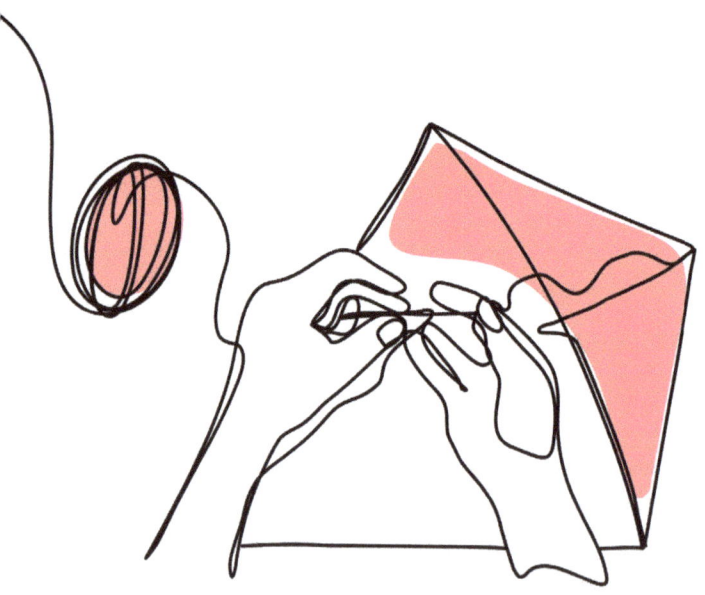

*Maybe then I will be able to build a kite
and run after my dreams...
carried by the kite in the clouds.*